K
JA 100 BRITISH ISLES
1908–2008

KHALSA JATHA BRITISH ISLES 1908–2008

by

Bhupinder (Peter) Singh Bance, Sukhbinder Singh Paul
& Gurpreet Singh Anand

An Introduction to Sikhism by

Amarpal Singh Sidhu

The Central Gurdwara (Khalsa Jatha) London
2008

First published by The Central Gurdwara (Khalsa Jatha) London, 2008
The Central Gurdwara, 62 Queensdale Road, London W11 4SG
Registered Charity No: 258324

© Peter Bance, Sukhbinder Singh Paul, Gurpreet Singh Anand & Amarpal Singh Sidhu 2008

ISBN 978-0-9560586-0-7
A catalogue record for this book is available from the British Library.

Design by Juga Singh (GRFIK.COM)
Printed in England, by RCS Plc.

ILLUSTRATIONS
Jacket photographs (front, top): Central Gurdwara London, 2008 (Jasprit Singh); (Bottom):
Sikh Prayers at Maharajah Bhupinder Singh Dharamsala, 1934 (Getty Images); (Back, left):
Sikhs outside 79 Sinclair Road, c. 1957 (Abinash Singh Taak); (right): Maharajah Bhupinder
Singh of Patiala, c. 1912 (Peter Bance).

Contents

Foreword

Dear Khalsa Jatha British Isles

It is with great pleasure that I write to congratulate you on the compilation of the history of the Khalsa Jatha British Isles and on the occasion of the Jatha's one hundred years since its founding in 1908.

A century in the life of any institution is a great occasion. Today our people are well established in British society. In 1908 however, the pioneers were struggling to find a foothold in an alien country. In such a situation, an organization was established which represented the collective hopes and aspirations of these pioneers, and more so one that helped preserve the spirit of the Khalsa alongside this struggle.

For me it is an added pleasure to be writing to you, as my Grandfather Maharaja Bhupinder Singh Ji contributed to the first building to house this institution, which the Sangat kindly named after him as 'the Maharaja Bhupinder Singh Dharamsala'.

May I congratulate the Sikh Sangat at large on this happy occasion and may I wish our community well in the years to come. By the grace of Akal Purakh, the Sikhs in which ever walk of life they may have chosen, are well established in the United Kingdom today. May Waheguru add further to this prosperity in the coming years and shower his blessings on the generations that follow.

This book I am sure will educate those who are not aware of the history of the community in Britain and who must remember today, the debt they owe to those pioneers, whose struggle paved the way for the Sikhs to finally emerge as one of the respected pillars of British society.

With best wishes
Yours sincerely

Maharaja Amarinder Singh
Motibagh Palace, Patiala, Punjab
8th October 2008

Preface

It gives me great pleasure to a write a preface for such a book, covering the history of the first 100 years of the Khalsa Jatha British Isles, which coincides with the auspicious occasion of the 300th anniversary of the Guru Gaddi of *Guru Granth Sahib* Ji.

On a personal note, I have a long-standing relationship with the Khalsa Jatha, having myself settled in the UK from India, and serving the Khalsa Jatha both as a Granthi and, more recently, as President.

I would like to extend heartfelt gratitude to the specially commissioned members of the sub-committee, consisting of Bhupinder (Peter) Singh Bance, Bhupinder Singh Bhasin, Sukhbinder Singh Paul, Amarpal Singh Sidhu and Gurpreet Singh Anand, formed for this purpose.

This book makes compelling reading and is a fitting testament to the founding fathers of the Khalsa Jatha. It is hoped that this book will be a valuable resource for future generations and for the wider community for years to come.

Waheguru Ji Ka Khalsa
Waheguru Ji Ki Fateh

Bhai Bhagwant Singh
President (Khalsa Jatha British Isles)
8 October 2008

Introduction *to* Sikhism

by Amarpal Singh Sidhu

WHO ARE THE SIKHS?

The relatively short history of the Sikhs has been a dynamic one, from 1499 when Guru Nanak's revolutionary teachings were revealed to the world, to the compilation of the writings of the Gurus in the *Adi Granth*, to the formation of the *Khalsa* – the culmination of 200 years of teachings of the Gurus – through to the present day. From the outset, when Guru Nanak began to spread his message, the spirit embodied in the Sikhs has been one of strength of faith. The concept of 'Chardi Kala' – to remain positive and in 'high spirits' – is central to Sikh philosophy. It is the simple and universal message of the Gurus that has stood the test of time.

Sikhs are known as hard-working, God-loving people who have made an impact in each and every community in which they have settled. To those who served alongside Sikhs in the two world wars, they are brave soldiers; to others they are hard-working farmers or retailers or professionals such as doctors and accountants. The Sikhs have become prominent members of the world religious landscape not merely because of their unique identity, but because they have held close the teachings of the Gurus, whose divinely revealed teachings are kept alive today within the Sikh Holy Scripture, the *Guru Granth Sahib Ji*.

THE MESSAGE OF GURU NANAK

Guru Nanak, the founder of the Sikh faith, was born in 1469 into a Hindu family in the village of Talwandi. Nanak lived in an age and society full of problems. Superstition, inequality, religious bigotry and fanaticism and the low status of women had very much weakened society. The caste system had divided the community. People of a lower caste were afforded little respect by higher-caste people. Women had little role to play in society. The practice of suttee, the burning to death of widows, was also firmly established.

Nanak grew up to reject the beliefs of his time and began preaching a universal message firmly based on equality, love, the brotherhood of mankind and the full emancipation of all members of the community. He preached the Oneness of God, the rejection of idol worship and the equality of men and women. Salvation is dependent on acceptance of the divine will as well as a person's actions, deeds and thoughts. Most importantly, salvation was open to all people irrespective of caste or creed. These were revolutionary beliefs in an age when each religion preached a monopoly on the ultimate truth.

At the age of 30, in the year 1499, Guru Nanak made four great journeys to preach this new message to the world. Guru Nanak's first journey took him to the east, as far as Assam. His second journey took him south, to Ceylon. His third journey took him northwards into the Central Asian Republics, as far as Tashkent. The fourth and longest journey was westwards, as far as Mecca and Jerusalem.

THE EVERYDAY PHILOSOPHY OF SIKHISM

Everywhere he travelled, Guru Nanak saw people blindly following the dogmas and rituals of their religion and neglecting the true meaning of religion. Guru Nanak discouraged these practices, instead preaching a practical message for everyday life that can be summed up in the following three teachings:

Naam Japna – remember God at all times. Naam is the living presence of the one, formless God as opposed to Maya, which is the world which we can see and touch. The Sikh way of life brings the Naam into our everyday lives. The only command in the Sikh scripture is 'Jap'. This means 'repeat, remember, and understand'. When we Jap we say 'yes' to God, we say 'yes' to life.

Kirat Karna – earning an honest living without greed and the exploitation of others. The Gurus promoted the life of a householder and placed great importance on the family. The Gurus themselves married and had families. At the time there were many who would abandon the world to try to find God, but the Sikh teaching is that God is realised by living within society.

View of the Golden Temple causeway, Amritsar c. 1870

Vund Chukna – sharing with others and helping those who are in need. The concept of *Seva* is very important within the Sikh way of life.

The foundations that Guru Nanak laid were built upon by the nine Gurus who succeeded him. Guru Angad introduced the Gurmukhi-script alphabet and expanded the institution of Guru Ka Langar (com-

Guru Nanak with his companion Mardana and a devotee. c. 1830 Punjab Plains School

munity kitchen) which had been begun by Guru Nanak. Guru Amardas trained a band of 146 apostles (52 were women) called Masands and sent them all round the country to preach Sikhism. Guru Ram Das established Amritsar as a centre for the Sikh faith and Guru Arjan compiled the *Adi Granth*, the Sikh Holy Scripture and installed it in the Harmandir Sahib (Golden Temple) in Amritsar.

It was during Guru Arjan's time that the universal appeal and rapid acceptance of Sikhism by large sections of the population began to alarm the Mughal emperors, the Muslim rulers of India. Both Hindus and Muslims were turning towards the new faith. In the year 1606, the Mughal Emperor Jahangir ordered the torture and martyrdom of Guru Arjan.

The sixth Guru, Guru Har Gobind, then raised an army to protect those being oppressed and introduced the concept of *miri-piri*. Guru Har Rai was known for healing with herbal medicines and Guru Har Krishen, the youngest of the Gurus helped to care for the sick and dying.

The oppression of non-Muslims grew with time, reaching its culmination in the reign of the Emperor Aurungzeb. Fired with religious zeal and an ambition to convert the whole of India to Islam, Aurungzeb introduced the Jizya tax (a tax on non-Muslims as prescribed by the Qur'an) and organised a campaign for the destruction of Hindu temples. In Kashmir, systematic forced conversion of Hindus to Islam began. When Guru Tegh Bahadhur, the ninth Guru, was approached by representatives of the Kashmiri Hindu community for help, he decided to make a stand against this oppression. He was martyred on the orders of Aurungzeb on 11 November 1675. This sacrifice by a religious leader was a unique act in that the Guru had given his own life for the freedom of people of another religion, so that they could practise their own beliefs.

Guru Gobind Singh, the tenth Guru, continued the fight against oppression. On the occasion of *Vaisakhi* 1699 he called a gathering of Sikhs at Anandpur Sahib and called for volunteers who would sacrifice themselves for the Guru. Five men stepped forward and were initiated by the Guru as the 'five beloved ones'. They represented the Khalsa, the brother/sisterhood of the pure. Remarkably, the Guru then bowed down in front of the five and asked them to initiate him into the Khalsa.

THE GURU GRANTH SAHIB

The Sikh scripture is called *Guru Granth Sahib*. It contains almost 6,000 verses written by the Sikh Gurus in their lifetimes and also verses from followers of other faiths, including both Hindu and Muslim saints. The first copy was compiled by Guru Arjan, the fifth Guru, 1604 and was formally installed in Harmandir Sahib, Amritsar the same year. This first version is still available at Kartarpur in the Punjab. Later, Guru Gobind Singh, the tenth Sikh Guru, completed it by adding the hymns of the ninth Guru. In 1708 he assembled his followers and ordained that after his death the Sikhs should consider the Granth their eternal Guru and receive instruction from it on all occasions. Right from the time of Guru Nanak it had been preached that the Guru of the Sikhs was the 'Word'; the passing on of the Guruship to the scripture was thus a final act of impersonalisation on the part of the living Guru. He declared that the Guru's spirit would henceforth reside in the Granth and the physical body of the Guru would be symbolically merged in the Guru Khalsa Panth, the Sikh congregation.

The Granth occupies a prominent place in Sikh congregations and is considered to represent the presence of the Guru through the 'Word' (*Shabad*). Sikh philosophy does not permit 'person Gurus' and therefore nobody can claim to be a Guru of the Sikhs in human form. Anyone who can read *Gurmukhi* can read the scriptures and no priest is necessary to conduct any service. The Granth is ceremoniously opened in the morning for service and similarly ceremoniously closed at the end of the day. The Sikh service consists of reading or singing the hymns and explanations of the spiritual content of the *Shabad.*

STRUCTURE & CONTENT OF THE GURU GRANTH SAHIB

The *Guru Granth Sahib* is unique in many ways. It was written by the Gurus themselves during their lifetimes and the verses bear the running totals of the number of *Shabads* in each section. The whole *Guru Granth Sahib* is written in poetry from beginning to end and runs to 1,430 pages. It is non-sectarian and includes poetry from both Hindu and Muslim saints, and represents the highest human value of the truth of the different religious beliefs of the world.

Although a range of languages (Panjabi, Hindi, Sindhi, Marathi, Gujarati, Brij, Sanskrit, Persian, Arabic etc.) is represented in the *Guru Granth Sahib*, the script used is Gurmukhi. The total number of hymns in the *Guru Granth Sahib* is 5,763. The poetry of the *Guru Granth Sahib* preaches worship of God (with the exclusion of all else), elimination of social evils, just governance, service to humanity, social equality of the sexes, simplicity, modesty and religious tolerance. The *Guru Granth Sahib* also questions the prevalent religious beliefs of the time, condemning needless rituals and customs. Matters relating to daily life and the continuous spiritual development of the human soul are a recurring theme throughout the *Guru Granth Sahib*.

ROLE OF THE GURDWARA

The very early Sikh temples, where Sikhs could come to hear the teachings of the Guru and sing devotional hymns, were called *Dharamsalas*. The name *Gurdwara*, meaning 'Gateway to the Guru' was first coined by the sixth Guru, Guru Hargobind. Any place where the *Guru Granth Sahib* is kept with all respect due to it can be called a Gurdwara, even a room in one's house.

The Sikh Gurus laid great emphasis on preaching against the many evils that afflicted Indian society of the time. The Gurdwara is open to all members of society, rich or poor, male and female. This feeling of equality is fostered by the *sangat* sitting together on the floor during the service. Instead of a priestly class, any member of the *sangat* can head the Sikh service and prayers, including reading from the *Guru Granth Sahib*. Social equality and communal service is emphasised

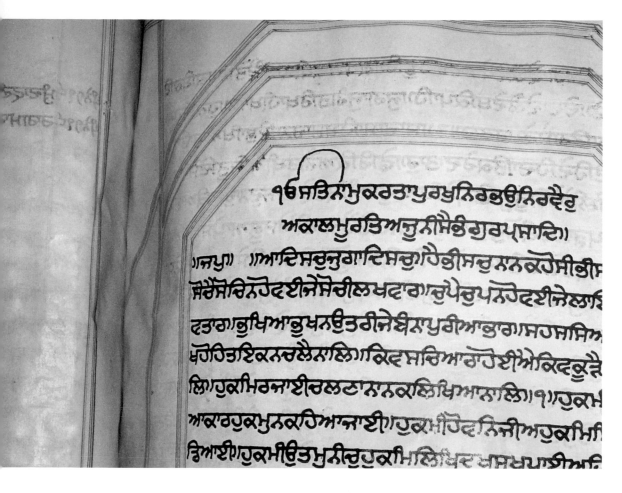

Opening page of an early handwritten copy of
the Guru Granth Sahib, 18th Century

in the service of *langar*, where free food for all is served and eaten together in a spirit of togetherness.

Over the years, the Gurdwara has continued to evolve so as to serve the Sikh community, with education in the forefront. Punjabi language classes are organised to teach children their mother tongue and the language used for the *Guru Granth Sahib*. A library of Sikh literature and books is often present. Many Gurdwaras organise *gurmat* camps during the summer months, enabling children to learn more about their faith and socialise with other Sikh children. *Kirtan* classes, the singing of hymns with musical instruments, are organised for young and old. The Gurdwara also acts as a meeting place and social centre for the elderly. As time goes on, more social services are continually being added to serve the ever-changing needs of the community.

The Founding of the Khalsa Jatha British Isles

by Peter Bance

From the middle of the nineteenth century to the beginning of the First World War, several hundred Sikhs came to Britain, ranging from long-term visitors, such as *lascars* and *ayahs* to short-term visitors such as students, soldiers, politicians to Indian royalty, and thus formed the beginning of Sikh migration to Britain. Although the arrival of many of these Sikhs was only intended to be a temporary arrangement, many ended up staying longer than they had anticipated, as opportunities presented themselves. Some, such as Professor Ganga Singh,[1] would change themselves by relaxing their religious duties and values so as to adapt to the British way of life, while the likes of Teja Singh would change and challenge the establishment to accommodate their Sikh faith.

By the turn of the century, a large proportion of this early migration of Sikhs was students, the children of aristocratic and influential Punjabi families from India. From these students, together with a handful of professional Sikhs in Britain, came the demand for and the establishment of a central Sikh body.

The history of the Central London Gurdwara's operating body, the Khalsa Jatha British Isles, goes back to 1906 when Teja Singh of District Gujranwlala was baptised by Sant Attar Singh Mastuana. In that same year Teja Singh and four other young men, Dharamanant Singh, Amar Singh, Hari Singh and Bhagat Singh, were sent to England by Sant Attar Singh to spread Sikhism. The young men left Bombay by sea on 6 August 1906 and reached London on 24 August. This group of five was fully sponsored by Sant Attar Singh for the dual purpose of receiving higher education and spreading the message of the Gurus in the Western hemisphere, where Sikhs had now begun to settle in

Teja Singh Mastuana, c. 1908

significant numbers.

On reaching Britain, Teja Singh joined University College London to study for the degree of Doctor of Sciences and also started to attend lectures at the Teachers' Training College. He attended university wearing his turban, unmindful of the stares of others, and wished that other Sikhs in Britain would also retain their long hair and turbans. Many of the handful of Sikh students and officials who were in Britain had shaved off their hair and beards. Teja Singh took upon himself the task of bringing them back into the Khalsa fold. However, he had barely completed the first semester when he learned that Cambridge University had not allowed a Sikh student to attend classes wearing his turban, because at Cambridge all students were required to wear a cap and a gown. During the next term Teja Singh took up the challenge and sought admission to the Science Tripos at Downing College, Cambridge on 22 January 1907,[2] formally enrolling at the University on 28 January 1907 as an affiliated student from the University of Punjab.[3] Teja Singh was able to convince the authorities of the significance of hair, the turban and other symbols for the Sikhs, thus gaining a concession for himself and for any other Sikh wishing to join the University, and became the first turbaned Sikh at Cambridge University.

Teja Singh spent a year and a half studying at Downing College, having entered for the intercollegiate examination in Natural Sciences in the Easter term of 1908, but he withdrew before the exams began.[4] As a student, he preached the tenets of the Gurus to fellow students in the town[5] and a small congregation was formed which met regularly at his residence every Sunday. Several Sikh students studying in England used to attend the hymns where *kirtan* and exegesis of *Gurbani* were generally held. Thus, the 'Khalsa Jatha British Isles' was founded in 1908.[6] Teja Singh continued his preaching work and regularly gave talks on the subject of Sikhism, the crowds growing and venues becoming more and more grand. On 17 January 1910, Teja Singh gave a seminar on 'The Mission of Guru Nanak and Guru Gobind Singh' at London's Westminster Palace Hotel[7] to celebrate the anniversary of Guru Gobind Singh.[8] The previous year the day had been marked with a meeting at Caxton Hall to mark 'Guru Gobind Singh Day' where leaflets entitled *Bande Mataram, Khalsa* were distributed to awaken the Sikhs from British rule.[9]

Among the chief founding members of the Khalsa Jatha, along with Teja Singh, were **Sardar Narain Singh Sargodha**,[10] a barrister-at-law, who became the first secretary of the Khalsa Jatha British Isles; and **Hardit Singh Malik**,[11] who had come to Britain with his family in 1908, at the age of 13 and was studying at a prep school in Notting

Sardar Narain Singh Sargodha, c. 1912

Hardit Singh Malik in his Royal Flying Corps
uniform, c. 1918

Hill. After a spell at Bristol's Clifton College and at Eastbourne College, Hardit Singh won a scholarship to Balliol College, Oxford. He took a keen interest in the running of the Khalsa Jatha, in between becoming the first Indian in the Royal Flying Corps in 1917 and fighting in France with the 28th Squadron in the Great War.[12] On his return to Britain, he served for a while as President of the Khalsa Jatha before heading back to India, later returning to work as an Indian civil servant at London's India House.

Hardit Singh's brother, Sardar Bahadur **Sir Teja Singh Malik** CIE, was also an active Sikh student and member of the Khalsa Jatha while studying at University College London and before leaving in 1910.[13]

The prominent students and residents who were part of the Khalsa Jatha during its early years were **Ganda Singh Oberoi** from Sialkot; barristers **Labh Singh** and **Nihal Singh,** both from Amritsar; **Sukhbir Singh Malik**; **Jaswant Singh Malik**; **Karam Singh Ramgarhia** from Amritsar; **Teja Singh Randhawa**; **Atma Singh**; **Ujjagar Singh** from Patiala; **Sher Singh Captain, Hardial Singh Gumdoor** from Patiala; and scholar **Kahan Singh Nabha**.

CHAPTER 2

Maharajah Bhupinder Singh at the Savoy Hotel,
C. 1920

The Maharajah Bhupinder Singh Dharamsala

by Peter Bance

It was resolved by the Khalsa Jatha British Isles that each member would subscribe £1 each month towards the funds for running the Khalsa Jatha,[1] and also that a permanent base must be sought in the UK from where the Khalsa Jatha could operate, and which would serve as a Gurdwara with the installation of a *Guru Granth Sahib*.

A lease on a house at Putney in London was sought and in 1911 Sardar Narain Singh of Sargodha was sent to India by the Khalsa Jatha to collect funds to acquire the premises. In India he attended and appealed to the Sikh Education Conference at Rawalpindi, where the *sangat* wholeheartedly donated the much-needed funds.

Sardar Narain Singh returned to England after a successful two months in India, during which time His Highness Maharajah Bhupinder Singh, the ruler of the principality of Patiala, was visiting England. The dashing Maharajah Bhupinder Singh was a well-travelled man but, unlike many Indian princes of the time who had adopted western values, Bhupinder Singh never sacrificed his Sikh ideology or Sikh appearance and, as the sovereign of the largest Sikh state, was looked upon with high regard by the Sikh people, who even referred to him as the head of the Sikhs. He was an accomplished sportsman, playing both tennis and hockey, and was an excellent cricket player, being instrumental in popularising the game in India.

It was while he was leading the Indian cricket team on a 'Tour of England' that was coupled with the coronation celebrations of King George V and Queen Mary in June 1911, which he attended, that the Maharajah met with a student delegation from the Khalsa Jatha British Isles and a number of Sikh military officers who were stationed at Hampton Court Palace for the coronation processions.

Max Arthur Macauliffe, c. 1910

wood in the Park, from Tuesday, July 11, until Friday, July 14, for Brigade training.

PROPOSED SIKH CHURCH IN LONDON.

A deputation of the British branch of the Khalsa Jatha and of military officers from Hampton Court has waited on his Highness the Maharaja of Patiala to urge upon him the necessity of having a Dharmsalla (Sikh Church) in the metropolis, and for that purpose to request him, on behalf of the Sikh community, to perform a preliminary ceremony in commemoration of the Coronation of their Majesties. The Maharaja acceded to the request, and promised a donation of £8,000 towards the project.

THE ROYAL SANITARY INSTITUTE CONGRESS.—The Lord Lieutenant of Ireland and Lady Aberdeen will attend the opening of the Congress of the Royal Sanitary Institute at Belfast on July 24.

Notice from The Times 3 July 1911

The Sikh officers and students informed the Maharajah of the need for a Dharamsala in London which would serve as a rest home for Sikh visitors and also as a place of worship for them. On behalf of the Sikh community, they requested him to perform a preliminary ceremony in commemoration of the coronation of Their Majesties. The Maharajah acceded to the request. With a princely donation from the ruler of Patiala, a house in Putney was taken on a 99-year lease and officially opened for use, being named appropriately 'The Maharajah Bhupinder Singh Dharamsala'. According to *The Times* newspaper, the Maharaja promised a donation of £8,000 towards the project.[2]

The house at Putney had a special room set aside to house the *Guru Granth Sahib*, where a weekly *deewan* was held on Sundays. There was no priest, so all duties were performed by the Sikh students and residents. The Maharajah maintained strong links with the Dharamsala and whenever he was Britain he would visit it from his London base at the Savoy Hotel. The exact location of the house, or even the name of the street in Putney, are not known, as the old records were not maintained; its existence is now known only by word of mouth.

In 1913, Maharajah Bhupinder Singh was in London on a shopping spree that included the purchase of seven Rolls Royce Silver Ghosts. Together with Teja Singh, who had returned from a spell in the United States, he obtained a 64-year lease on a large, three-storey house at 79 Sinclair Road in Shepherds Bush, West London that would serve as a Gurdwara.[3] Maharajah Bhupinder Singh Patiala also visited the Gurdwara in 1930 when he came to the Round Table Conference in London (a series of conferences held to discuss India's call for independence from British rule), regularly attending Sunday prayers at the Gurdwara. Teja Singh remained as President of the Gurdwara during

Right: Maharajah Bhupinder Singh Dharamsal
79 Sinclair Road, London, c. 19

Next Page: Langar Room at Maharaja
Bhupinder Singh Dharamsal
79 Sinclair Road, 19

the whole time he was in Britain and resided within the confines of the Dharamsala. It is said that Teja Singh carried out the first *Amrit parchaar* in England at 79 Sinclair Road, and many Sikhs who had previously been relaxed in their practices became inclined towards Sikhism.

Among the 1913 committee was the renowned Sikh scholar Kahn Singh Nabha, who was in the service of Maharajah Hira Singh of Nabha state. Kahn Singh visited Britain at the invitation of the celebrated writer Max Arthur Macauliffe; he had first met him in 1885 at Rawalpindi and this led to a life-long friendship. Macauliffe sought a great deal of advice and guidance from Kahn Singh for the work he was then preparing on the Sikh scriptures and for the history of Sikhism that he was writing. Macauliffe took Kahn Singh with him to England when his six volumes on *The Sikh Religion* were printed at Oxford's Clarendon Press in 1907. Such was his admiration for Kahn Singh that he assigned the copyright in the book to him and also offered him one of his houses in England. On the opening of Sinclair Road in 1913, shortly before his death on 15 March, the renowned author, Sikh historian and scholar paid a visit to the Dharamsala, a visit that he mentions in his letters.

The Khalsa Jatha thought it proper that the management of the institution and its funds should be entrusted to a representative Sikh society in India. Consequently a scheme was prepared and passed at its meeting of 12 October 1913, the aim of which was to create an association under the name of Guru Khalsa Foreign Mission. It was laid down in the scheme that a provisional committee of seven members should be elected to arrange the preliminaries, and that a provisional committee should constitute the first executive committee of the Guru Khalsa Foreign Mission.[4]

At the Khalsa Jatha's meeting of 4 April 1914 some changes were made and passed, whereby an Executive Committee was appointed consisting of seven members, with Teja Singh as President and Sardar Man Singh as Secretary. The Khalsa Jatha subsequently resolved, at its meeting of 10 May 1914, that all powers and privileges of the Khalsa Jatha British Isles be given to the 'Guru Khalsa Foreign Mission'. Consequently all surplus funds of the Jatha were transferred to the Guru Khalsa Foreign Mission. The Khalsa Jatha became Europe's main Sikh body and represented Western hemisphere Sikhs in political and religious causes, as in 1914, when the British demolished a part of the wall at the historic Gurdwara at Rakabganj Sahib, New Delhi. On that occasion Khalsa Jatha sent a written deputation to the British government to give its views.

By now, the Khalsa Jatha British Isles had over a hundred Sikh stu-

Hymn singing with a dholaki and vaaja at the Maharajah Bhupinder Singh Dharamsala, c. 1930

dents, and it organised a committee of two Sikh students to go to ports and stations to welcome newly arriving Sikhs to the country and direct them to the Gurdwara. In this way all newly arrived Sikhs would be aware of the Gurdwara, and in return the Gurdwara would support them and help them to settle in the UK.

The Maharajah Bhupinder Singh Dharamsala became a base for all Sikhs visiting and staying in England. Among them was a deputa-

tion from Canada consisting of Dr Nand Singh Seera, Balwant Singh and Narain Singh, who stayed at the Dharamsala for a few days en route to India to demonstrate against British rule. The Dharamsala also acted as a half-way house for Sikhs travelling to and from the USA and Canada. In 1924 a deputation journeying from Canada and the USA to participate in the *Jaito Morcha* in the Punjab stayed for a few days at the Maharajah Bhupinder Singh Dharamsala.[5]

Convalescent Sikh soldiers at Brighton, c. 1916

It was common during this time to observe that arriving Sikhs – especially the students, who were the offspring of wealthily Punjabi families – were very European in their attitudes and had either given up or become complacent about their Sikh practices. The opening of the Dharamsala encouraged them to reinsert themselves into the community and again follow the doctrines of Sikhism.

With the outbreak of war in 1914, the number of Sikh students declined and only a few remained to carry on the *Sewa*, but Britain saw a greater influx of Sikh arrivals in the form of Sikh soldiers fighting for the British Empire and returning from the Western Front in France.

The badly wounded Indian soldiers, of whom the vast majority were Sikhs, were sent to makeshift hospitals in England.[6] Among the most famous were Brighton's Royal Pavilion and the Dome, and York Place Hospital, while the Brighton Work House became the Kitchener General Indian Hospital. Other Indian hospitals were at Brockenhurst, Netley, Bournemouth, Milford-on-Sea, Barton-on-Sea, and Ashurst. At Brighton a marquee was erected in the Pavilion grounds to serve as a Gurdwara.

The convalescent Sikh soldiers had a strong desire to see the capital of the British Empire before they returned to the front, so the Secretary of State for India arranged with the military authorities for a regular succession of day excursions to London after the Christmas holidays of 1914. The convalescent soldiers visited in groups of twenty-four, and were taken round to see the principal streets and buildings. The visits included shopping trips to Selfridges and a ride on London's underground.[7]

On 23 December 1914, in connection with the celebration of the 248th birthday of Guru Gobind Singh, *The Times* newspaper reported that: a party of Sikh officers and soldiers, convalescing from their wounds, travelled to London from a hospital at Burton, near Milton, in the New Forest. They were met at Waterloo Station by leading members of the Khalsa Jatha British Isles, and taken past St Paul's to the Tower where they saw the regalia. They were also shown Whitehall, the Houses of Parliament, Buckingham Palace and Hyde Park on their way to the 'Khalsa Headquarters' in Sinclair Road, West Kensington, where Mr. C. H. Roberts, M.P., the Under-Secretary for India, and Lady Cecilia Roberts entertained them at an Indian dinner. In the afternoon they attended the celebration of their Guru's birthday at Caxton Hall, being enthusiastically received by the large number of English and Indian friends assembled to meet them which included Princess Sophia Duleep Singh, the granddaughter of Shere-Punjab Maharajah Ranjit Singh.[8] This was followed by the writer Sant Nihal Singh giving an outline of the life and teaching of Guru Gobind Singh, with Major Thakore Singh of the 47th Sikh Regiment speaking in Hindi on behalf of the visiting Sikh soldiers and thanking their Sikh brothers from the Khalsa Jatha for so kindly arranging the celebration. Princess Sophia Duleep Singh, the youngest of Maharajah Duleep Singh's three daughters with Maharani Bamba, had much affection for her father's countrymen and nursed many of the wounded Indians in the makeshift hospitals. She was also an occasional visitor to the Maharajah Bhupinder Singh Dharamsala at Sinclair Road during her life.

CHAPTER 3

Sikh worshipper rolling flour to prepare
chapatties for the langar at the Maharajah
Bhupinder Dharamsala, c. 1938

1920 – 1939

by Peter Bance

In 1920 a Sikh deputation of Sewaram Singh, Shivdev Singh Uberoi, Sohan Singh Rawalipindi and Ujjal Singh arrived in England to press the claim of the Sikh community in India for increased representation on legislative bodies. The party was supported by the Khalsa Jatha during its stay, although its mission in England was not a success and it was informed that the Government of India did not acquiesce to its claim, a member of the deputation stated 'We shall return home with an impression that justice denied us in India is unobtainable even in England'.[1]

Sardar Shiv Dev Singh Uberoi became an eminent member of the Khalsa Jatha British Isles and, on his death in England in 1932, a message of condolence was received from the King and Queen. His funeral service at Golders Green Crematorium was attended by Lieutenant-Colonel Stewart Patterson, representing the Secretary of State for India and Mr W. D. Croft, Sir F. Stewart, the Permanent Under-Secretary for India, and Khalsa Jatha members including Rewal Singh, Diwan Singh and Manmohan Singh.[2]

Sikh student Manmohan Singh was an active Khalsa Jatha member. He had come to England to train as a civil engineer and in 1936 received his BSc degree from the University of Bristol. While in England he also completed a two-year course in flying and aeronautical engineering, for which he had been given a scholarship by the Government of India. He later held many flying records.[3] During the Second World War he was one of five Sikhs among a total of twenty-four Indian Air Force pilots sent to Britain in September 1940.

The early 1920s saw a shift not only in the numbers of Sikhs arriving in Britain, but also in the type of Sikh men arriving. Young Pun-

jabi men from Jullandhar, Hoshiarpur and Ludhiana[4] began making
the slow and steady trek to Britain for work.[5] But this crucial period
witnessed the arrival of a larger influx of a small, close-knit Sikh community, mainly of West Punjab. This distinct group of fully bearded,
turbaned men were 'Bhat Sikhs', more familiarly known as 'Bhatras'.
They became itinerant traders, selling ready-made clothes and house-
hold goods door to door, and settled around the East End of London.
The next thirty years saw the Bhat Sikhs assume a prominent role at
the Dharamsala, being the larger part of the community at the time.

One of the earliest Sikh families to arrive in Britain was that of Dr
Diwan Singh, a freedom fighter for the Independence of India, who
arrived in Edinburgh in 1931 with his wife and children. He became a
central figure in the Khalsa Jatha British Isles and was effectively the
representative of Sikhs in Britain throughout the 1930s and 1940s and
President of the Khalsa Jatha for much of this time.[6] By the late 1930s,
the Sikh population's demographics in Britain began to see a dramat-
ic change, with the arrival of Sikh women. The Dharamsala became

Two Sikhs preparing batter for puri in the
kitchen at Sinclair Road, 19

Sikh pedlar at work, c. 1930

very much family oriented and a Sikh woman often conducted the Sunday services and certain ceremonies.

The year 1932 saw the arrival of long-serving *Sewadar* Sardar Asa Singh Grewal, who had been in the British Indian Army and had previously visited Britain in the 1920s. The name of Asa Singh became synonymous with his long years of dedicated service at the Maharajah Bhupinder Singh Dharamsala, where he served the congregation continually for almost forty years. He effectively spent all his time in whatever capacity was required, from cooking the *langar*, to mending a leaking roof, to changing a dripping tap at the Dharamsala. He died on 29 December 1968, only a few months before the Gurdwara at Sinclair Road closed and moved to its new site at 62 Queensdale Road.[7]

In 1927, after spending a year at Oxford, Hardit Singh Malik joined the Indian Civil Service, returning later to England as the Deputy High Commissioner. In 1934 his duties in London's India House came to an end and the Khalsa Jatha invited its former President for a farewell get-together with guests including Princess Sophia Duleep Singh.

The year 1934 also saw the future prominent author, historian and writer Khushwant Singh arriving in England as a law student at Kings College London. Son of the wealthy Delhi property tycoon Sir Sobha Singh, Khushwant Singh qualified as a barrister from the Inner Temple. It was in Britain that he courted his future wife, Kaval Malik, the niece of Air Force pilot Hardit Singh Malik.[10] On his arrival in Britain he stayed at the Dharamsala at Shepherds Bush, where he recalls running into a young man of his own age who was staying in the Gurdwara and getting two meals a day free of charge. Although he had only passed his matriculation examination, the young man was known as 'Gyani'. He was looking for a job in a factory or to become a pedlar, and if nothing better came his way, he would become the *Granthi* at the Gurdwara. Khushwant recalled: 'A few weeks later I heard the boy had hit the jackpot. He went to a dog race, laid a bet on one and won over five hundred pounds; a sizeable fortune in those times. When he returned to the Gurdwara, he spread out the currency notes on his bed and slept on them at night to symbolise his rolling in wealth. He moved out of the Gurdwara and found lodging in keeping with his new status. I lost track of him.' Khushwant left for India after his studies but returned to Britain in 1947 as a Public Relations Officer for the Indian High Commission in London. Surprisingly, he again met 'Gyani', who now 'was a peon, the lowest paid on the staff. Whatever little he earned, he staked at dog races. It was a mug's game but he could not take it out of his system. Gambling had got into his blood.'

The 1930s also witnessed a mixed congregation at the Maharajah Bhupinder Singh Dharamsala consisting of English men and women seated in the *Durbar* at Sinclair Road. Such occurrences were not

Left: Dr Diwan Singh and his wife, Mrs Kundan Kaur, c. 1930

Above: Flight Lt Hardit Singh Malik ICS. Farewell party with Princess Sophia Duleep Singh at the Maharaja Bhupinder Singh Dharamsala, London, 1934

Right to left, standing: Babu Singh, Pakher Singh, Balbir Singh Grewal, Mr Jain, ICS, G. S. Malik, Tarlok Singh,[8] Dr Ishar Singh Bhalla, Kartar Singh Upel, Banta Singh. **Centre row:** Dilbagh Singh, Rajinder Singh Batra, Bishan Singh,

...agar Singh, Ravinder H. Darshan Singh, G. N. ...tra, Harchand Singh, Sant Singh Kapur, H. S. ...ewal. **Seated at front**: Gurcharn Singh Malvai ...ecretary), Piara Singh Sahi, Basant Singh, Ram ...ngh Nehra, Princess Sophia Duleep Singh, Dr ...wan Singh (President), Hardit Singh Malik, ICS ...x-President), Manmohan Singh,[9] Uttam Singh ...ugal, Mr Puri. **Seated on floor**: Harbans Singh ...ssistant secretary), Sohan Singh, Gurbux ...ngh Choudhry.

Right: Asa Singh Grewal and his son Sajjan Singh

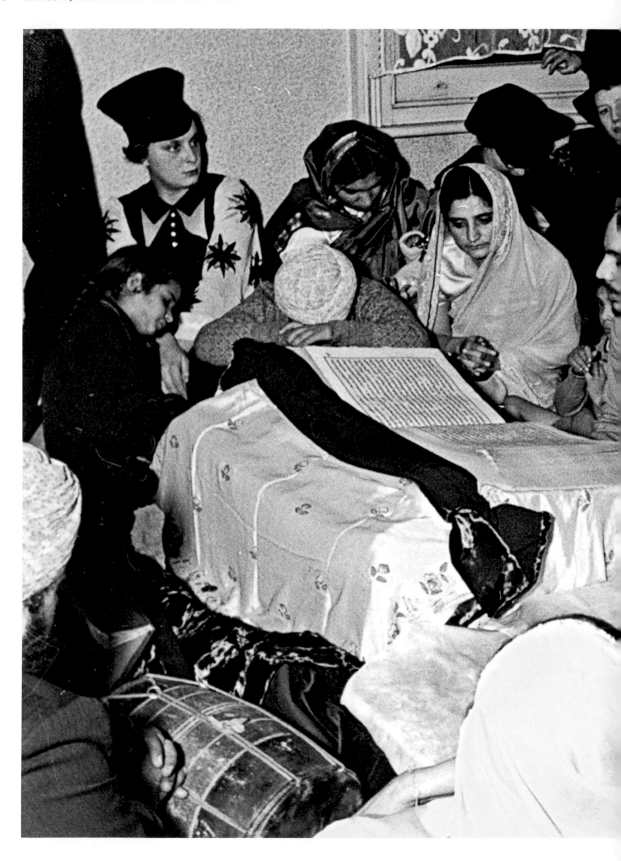

rare, and members of the English community were regularly seen participating at weekly prayers. In the early years after its founding, the Dharamsala attracted many Britons, possibly as a result of their links with the Raj in India, as many of them had grown up and lived in India as families of military servicemen.

In 1935 Sardar Bahadur Mohan Singh Rawalpindi, was appointed a member of the Council of the Secretary of State for India in London. He is seen here with his wife, Lajvanti, being welcomed by the Khalsa Jatha members Manmohan Singh, Harbans Singh (Assistant secretary) and Dr Dewan Singh (President) in 1935.

One of the most historic episodes in the Indian Freedom calendar also occurred in Britain during this period, involving the revolutionary Udham Singh. Udham Singh was reputedly a survivor of the Jallianwala Bagh Massacre at Amritsar in 1919, when General Reginald Dyer ordered his troops to open fire upon an unarmed crowd that included women and children. It became Udham Singh's mission in life, to one day avenge the killings of these innocent Indians, that drove him to Britain. There are many gaps in Udham Singh's life history, as he was a very secretive and private person. Official reports put his arrival in Britain at about 1933, travelling with a Pritam Singh from Patiala and forty other Indians on board a ship via the Suez Canal and Marseilles. On his arrival in London, Udham Singh stayed at the Indian Students Institute at Gower Street with Pritam Singh for two days and then moved to 79 Sinclair Road, where he stayed for a month at the Dharamsala.[11] Udham Singh never stayed in one place for long, frequently moving address, but he was constantly seen at Khalsa Jatha headquarters, where he lodged at times, or was seen bor-

Previous Page: Europeans sitting in the Durbar at 79 Sinclair Road, 1938

Left: Khalsa Jatha President Dr Diwan Singh greeting Sardar Bahadur Mohan Singh of Rawalpindi (standing on left), c. 1935

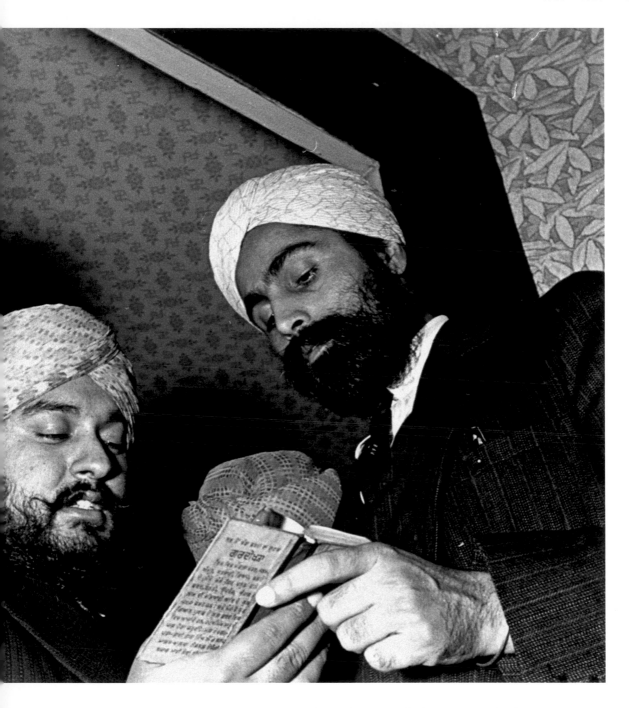

bove: Three Sikhs singing hymns from a Gutka
t Maharajah Bhupinder Singh Dharamsala,
938

rowing money from the *sangat* for his secretive deeds.

The Khalsa Jatha's tradition of using smart venues to celebrate Sikh anniversaries continued. The anniversary of the birth of Guru Gobind Singh was celebrated on the afternoon of 20 January 1937 with a tea party hosted at the Mayfair Hotel.[12] The President of the Khalsa Jatha at the time, Sardar Bahadur Mohan Singh, gave a talk on the life and work of Guru Gobind Singh, with guests Sir Louis Dane and Sir Mi-

chael O'Dwyer – both of whom would receive fatal wounds from bullets shot by Udham Singh three years later – in attendance.

During his time in England Udham Singh was engaged in the peddling business, using a small car for the purpose. On 11 October 1937,
British Intelligence identified him as an Indian revolutionary with as-
sociations with the Ghadar Party.[13] At the time he was residing at 14
Artillery Passage,[14] a common address for early Sikh migrants, and
was also well known among the Sikh pedlars who lived in the Midlands and in Southampton.[15]

The Maharajah Bhupinder Dharamsala, 79
Sinclair Road, London, January 1938

This gathering on the Anniversary of the Birth of the Tenth Sikh Guru, Guru Gobind Singh, was celebrated at 79 Sinclair Road. President Sardar Bahadur Mohan Singh is seated in the centre. The two middle rows consist of mainly Bhat Sikhs.[16] Udham Singh can be seen standing at the far back, behind the gentleman wearing a hat.

14. **Shaheed Udham Singh**, 15. Saudagar Singh Rathore, 20. Lal Singh Bhagat, 24. Nanak Singh Punjabi, 25. Nihal Singh Metola, 26. Wasti Singh, 27. Sant Singh Digwa, 28. Pushkar Singh, 29. Lahori Singh Landa, 30. Tehl Singh Digwa, 31. Daulat Singh Potiwal, 32. Professor Waryam Singh Thuthi, 34. Kesar Singh 'Raboota' Digwa, 35. Inder Singh, 37. Ranjit Singh Devi-Ditta, 39. Gopal Singh Suwali, 42. Mangal Singh Potiwal, 44. Asa Singh Grewal, 46. Meherban Singh Dhupia, 49. Kundan Kaur, 50. Sardar Bahadur Mohan Singh Rawalpindi, 51. Dr Diwan Singh, 52. Pakher Singh, 53. Kirpal Singh Sagoo, 54. Brigadier Labh Singh, 55. Wing Commander Basant Singh, 56. Khushwant Singh, 57. Jagjit Singh, 62. Gurbachan Singh, 63. Indarjit Singh, 64. Surinder Singh

CHAPTER 4

Jdham Singh, London, c. 1935

$$1940 - 1950$$

by Peter Bance

Udham Singh on his arrest at Caxton Hall, 1940

On 23 February 1940 former Khalsa Jatha President Sardar Bahadur Sardar Mohan Singh retired from his position as adviser to the Secretary of State for India and bid farewell to his countrymen at a party held for him at St James's Court Restaurant, where Princess Sophia Duleep Singh performed the ceremony of garlanding the guest of honour.[1]

Weeks later, Udham Singh was eying his revenge target. His initial target was General Reginald Dyer, who had led the soldiers who fired on the civilians in Amritsar in 1919, but Dyer had already died before Udham Singh's arrival in Britain. The next best target was the former Governor of the Punjab, Sir Michael O'Dwyer, who had given the orders for the massacre at Amritsar. On the morning of 13 March 1940 Udham Singh walked into Caxton Hall, where a meeting in the Tudor Hall was being held jointly by the East Indian Association and the Royal Central Asiatic Society. He fired bullets into Sir Michael O'Dwyer, Lord Zetland, Lord Lamington and Sir Louis Dane. O'Dwyer died instantly. On his arrest, Udham Singh gave his name to the police as 'Ram Mohammed Singh Azad', signifying the freedom of Hindu, Muslims and Sikhs. India's Congress members Gandhi and Nehru condemned his actions.

After the arrest and charging of Udham Singh, the Indians in London held a meeting at Commercial Road on 19 March 1940 to appoint a lawyer and to arrange a collection for his defence. A committee was formed with Krishna Menon (General Secretary of the Indian League) as Chairman, Dr Diwan Singh of the Khalsa Jatha as Adviser, Shiv Singh Johal (General Secretary of the Khalsa Jatha) as Cashier, Iqbal Khan BA, LLB (President of the Indian Workers Association), Ram Narayan

ASKE,
RICHMOND,
YORKSHIRE.

♛
Z

26. 3. 40.

Dear Eva,

So many thanks for
your sympathy and good
wishes. My ribs are healing
but are still tender. Other-
wise I am none the worse
and am playing golf!
I am certainly very lucky.
No one was more astonished

at learning that I was alive
than my would-be assassin,
for he said in Court : "Is
Zetland dead? He ought to
be, for I put two shots into
him here" - pointing to his
side. What he said was quite
true, and both bullets were
subsequently recovered from my
clothes which were not only
perforated but singed by the
flame of the pistol!
Love to all at Honey B. I
shall hope to see you ere
long.
              Yours aff
                    Lawrence

A letter by Lord Zetland, writing of his injuries
caused by Udham Singh's bullets , 26 March 1940

Sharma, Deen Mohamed, Noor Din Quereshi, and Didar Singh, along with Khalsa Jatha committee members Sant Singh Pardesi, Rewal Singh and Rattan Singh Shaad. The committee organised a lawyer and was affiliated with the US-based Ghadar Party. It carried out house-to-house visits to known Indians and collected £1,650 for Udham Singh's defence, with additional funds coming from the USA.[2]

In prison, Udham Singh regularly wrote to the Khalsa Jatha, addressing his letters to the Secretary, Shiv Singh Johal, at Sinclair Road and boasting that he was a guest of 'HM King George' now. His requests were simple and at times odd, ranging from a *Gutka*, a history book, a pair of trousers, to a copy of 'Heer Waris Shah' which he wished to take with him to court on which to take his oath. On 1 April 1940, Udham Singh was formally charged with the murder of Sir Michael O'Dwyer, and on 4 June 1940 he was committed to trial at the Old Bailey. He was found guilty and on 31 July 1940 was hanged at Pentonville Prison. All his personal property was sent to Shiv Singh Johal. The Khalsa Jatha made a request for the deceased's ashes on 6 August 1940 so that they could be taken back to India for last rites according to the Sikh religion. However, Shiv Singh Johal was informed that the personal effects and the books belonging to the Gurdwara would be returned, but not the ashes.

During the time leading up to Indian Independence, Khalsa Jatha President Dr Diwan Singh was continually speaking up for India's freedom and was visited by many revolutionaries, including an uncle and cousin of Subash Chandra Bose,[3] Bhagat Singh's uncle Sardar Ajit Singh, and Krishna Menon, while Udham Singh had been a regular visitor to Diwan Singh's house.[4]

During the Second World War many buildings near the Gurdwara were destroyed in the bombardment, but the Gurdwara was untouched. The Dharamsala remained open for the *sangat*, although many had fled back to India to be with their families, especially as the partition of India was now looming. The Khalsa Jatha Secretary, Sarwan Singh, remained and lived at the Dharamsala for the duration of the war. The Khalsa Jatha felt that it was best to remove the *Guru Granth Sahib* temporarily to a safer place, and it was decided that Dr Diwan Singh should take it to Birmingham, to his house at Bandywood Road. On *Gurpurabs* Diwan Singh would make special journeys from Birmingham with the *Guru Granth Sahib* for service at 79 Sinclair Road. According to his son, Indarjit Singh, a house in Birmingham's Balsall Heath was also used as a Gurdwara during the war, this being the house of Sant Singh Pardesi at 8 Belgrave Road, Birmingham 12.[5] A weekly *deewan* was held at Belgrave Road every Sunday during this time. Here, religious and social issues were also discussed and, after a

Khalsa Jatha Secretary Shiv Singh Johal, c. 1945

Sikh soldiers at Maharajah Bhupinder Singh
Dharamsala, Vaisakhi 1945

collection was made, a *Nishan Sahib* was erected outside and it was named 'Gurdwara Guru Nanak Mission Centre.' All *Akhand Paths* and *Gurpurabs* were held here, and *langar* was still served there for a full three days during prayers, even though a ration system was in place because of the war.[6] On *Vaisakhi* 1945, Sikh soldiers stationed in Britain joined the prayers and celebrations at the Maharajah Bhupinder Dharamsala, Sinclair Road.

Post Indian Independence

by Peter Bance

Post-War Secretary & President of Khalsa Jatha,
Gyani Rattan Singh Shaad, c. 1949

The Maharajah Bhupinder Singh Dharamsala was the stepping-stone to the opening of numerous Gurdwaras all over Britain. From the 1940s onwards it was common practice to hold prayers in the houses of established Sikh families, such as in Cardiff at Harnam Singh Koumi's house, Ipswich at Naranjan Singh Lovlee's house, Gravesend at Charan Singh Jandiali's house and Manchester at Bhil Singh Landa's house. There were similar patterns also for Birmingham, Edinburgh and Glasgow. Private houses continued to be the places of worship until such time as the communities had grown. They would then hire school halls or community centres to hold weekly *deewans*. This practice continued until communities could afford to purchase a Gurdwara premises, such as in Manchester, where the first Gurdwara was opened at 15 Monton Street in 1953.

The end of the Second World War saw the visit to England of India's leading revolutionary, famous for speaking up against the extortionate taxes on the Punjab farmers during the British Raj, Sardar Ajit Singh, the uncle of Shaheed Bhagat Singh.[1] An activist and a patriot, he escaped from India and the threat of British prosecution and was in Italy during the war. When an interim government in India was announced under Jawaharlal Nehru, Ajit Singh was allowed to return to his homeland and decided to stop in England en route.[2] He arrived in London via Hull on 10 January 1947 and a Welcoming Committee was formed, consisting primarily of Khalsa Jatha members Dr Diwan Singh, Sarwan Singh Chokal, Ram Singh and Rattan Singh Shaad, with the Indian League's Krishna Menon as the committee chairman, Dr Sukhdev Dutta, Professor S. Dara, Iqbal Khan of the Indian Workers Association, Mr Deen and Mr Patel.[3] Sardar Ajit Singh toured the

Sardar Ajit Singh visiting the Sikh community
at Khalsa Jatha British Isles, 1947. Ajit Singh is seated
behind the Guru Granth Sahib, with Khalsa Jatha
President Diwan Singh seated second to his left,
followed by Asa Singh Grewal.

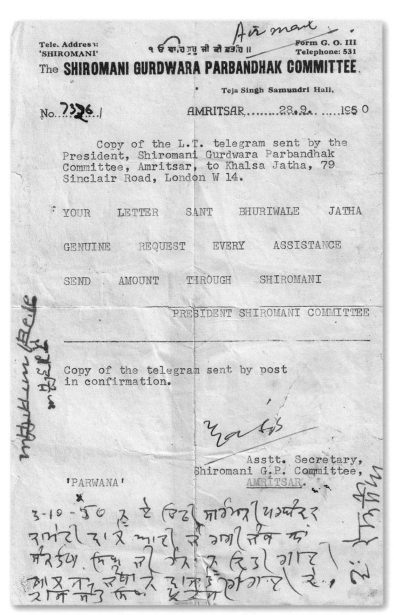

Right: SGPC letter to Khalsa Jatha to support
the collection for the construction of the
Parkarma at the Golden Temple

Sikh community, being taken around by Khalsa Jatha members Diwan Singh and Asa Singh Grewal, while at the India Office a Repub-
lic Day procession was held where Ajit Singh's supreme service was
honoured. Ajit Singh was invited to the Maharajah Bhupinder Singh
Dharamsala where an *Akhand Path* was performed for him and Dr
Diwan Singh presented him with £200 on behalf of the Khalsa Jatha.[4]

In 1947 Gyani Rattan Singh Shaad took the position of Secretary of
Khalsa Jatha British Isles. A political and religious activist, he had met
Udham Singh and known him for many years since his own arrival
to England in 1936, for a while sharing lodgings with him in Bedford.[5]
Rattan Singh later became the Khalsa Jatha President in 1951, when

he organised the first commemoration of the anniversary of Udham Singh at the Dharamsala, which was celebrated on the date of Udham Singh's hanging and became known as Shaheed Udham Singh Day.[6]

In the 1940s the Shiromani Gurdwara Prabandak Committee (SGPC) of Amritsar sought the services of Sant Puran Singh Bhuriwale for construction work at the Golden Temple.[7] This service included

Welcoming Party for the 'Sant Bhuriwale Jatha rear of Maharajah Bhupinder Singh Dharamsal London, August 1950

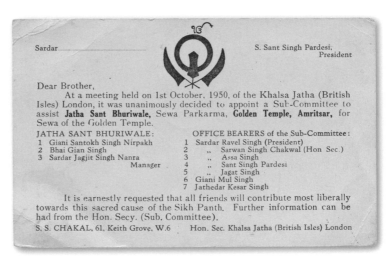

Sardar..   S. Sant Singh Pardesi,
President

Dear Brother,
At a meeting held on 1st October, 1950, of the Khalsa Jatha (British Isles) London, it was unanimously decided to appoint a Sub-Committee to assist **Jatha Sant Bhuriwale**, Sewa Parkarma, **Golden Temple, Amritsar**, for Sewa of the Golden Temple.

JATHA SANT BHURIWALE:
1 Giani Santokh Singh Nirpakh
2 Bhai Gian Singh
3 Sardar Jagjit Singh Nanra
                    Manager

OFFICE BEARERS of the Sub-Committee:
1 Sardar Ravel Singh (President)
2 „   Sarwan Singh Chakwal (Hon Sec.)
3 „   Assa Singh
4 „   Sant Singh Pardesi
5 „   Jagat Singh
6 Giani Mul Singh
7 Jathedar Kesar Singh

It is earnestly requested that all friends will contribute most liberally towards this sacred cause of the Sikh Panth. Further information can be had from the Hon. Secy. (Sub. Committee).
S. S. CHAKAL, 61, Keith Grove, W.6   Hon. Sec. Khalsa Jatha (British Isles) London

Right: Khalsa Jatha British Isles appealing to the community to donate generously, c. 1950

purchasing various buildings and properties from private individuals around the Golden Temple and constructing a wider marble walkway and four entrances at the holy shrine. Sant Puran Singh instructed a Jatha led by the Amritsar *Raagi*, Gyani Santokh Singh Nirpakh, together with Gian Singh Taak and Jagjit Singh Nanra to tour first the UK and then the United States and Canada, to raise money for the cause. Named the 'Sant Bhuriwale Jatha,' they arrived in England on 18 August 1950 and were met by their hosts, the Khalsa Jatha British Isles, and resided at the Maharajah Bhupinder Singh Dharamsala.

On 1 October 1950, at a meeting held at 79 Sinclair Road under the presidency of Sardar Sant Singh Pardesi, it was resolved that the Khalsa Jatha 'wholeheartedly supported the *sewa* undertaken by the visiting Jatha from the Golden Temple and requested their member and non member Sikhs, and also friends of the Sikh community to contribute to the cause'.[8] The Khalsa Jatha set up a sub-committee made up of Rawel Singh (President), Sant Singh Pardesi, Sarwan Singh Chakal (Honorary Secretary), Jagat Singh, Asa Singh Grewal, Giani Mul Singh and Jathedar Singh Kesar Singh to assist in the raising of contributions for the sacred cause.

After travelling the length of Britain, on 18 August 1951 the Jatha Sant Bhuriwale bade farewell to the Sikh community in Britain, having collected generous sums for the Golden Temple. The Jatha had served the *sangats* of London and its surrounding areas with their *shabad kirtans* during their stay, and upon their departure from the Maharajah Bhupinder Singh Dharamsala, the Khalsa Jatha British Isles under its President and Secretary, Sant Singh Pardesi and Sarwan Singh Chakal, presented the Bhuriwale Jatha with *saropas* and Gyani Santokh Singh Nirpakh with a ceremonial sword inscribed to him.

Gyani Santokh Singh Nirpakh returned to India with the Bhuri-

Above: Khalsa Jatha members awarding saropa and ceremonial sword to the Bhuriwale Jatha at 79 Sinclair Road, August 1951

Left: Sikhs outside the front entrance of the Maharajah Bhupinder Singh Dharamsala, c. 1957

Below: Sword presented to the Bhuriwale Jatha's head, Gyani Santokh Singh Niprakh

wale Jatha in 1951, but his services to the UK *sangat* were so much admired that the Khalsa Jatha invited him to return on a personal basis to serve the *sangat* with his sermons, and his services were secured by the Dharamsala from 1955.

Up to the early 1950s, the pattern of Europeans among the congregation of the Dharamsala continued, but owing to a lack of Sikh preaching outside the community the numbers gradually dwindled. There was even small group of white Sikhs who formed the Guru Ramdas Trust. In 1954 the services of a resident priest were procured

Sikh gathering at Maharajah Bhupinder Dharamsala, c. 1953

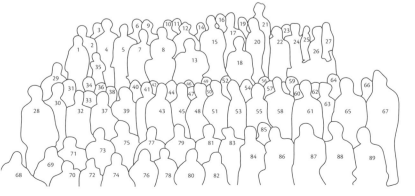

2. Sewa Singh, 3. Kesar Singh Raboota, 5. Inder Singh, 8. Swaran Singh Swali

(Nottingham), 13. Fateh Singh 'Dud' Taak. 17. Preetam Singh QC, 19. Sajjan Singh Grewal, 22. Harbans Singh Landa, 24. Piara Singh Bhaker, 28. Harbans Singh Bhaker (Preston), 31. Judge Choor Singh (Singapore), 33. Khazan Singh, 34. Subegh Singh (Kenya), 37. Gehna Singh Gola, 39. Hari Singh, 41. Pritam Singh Taak, 45. Asa Singh Grewal, 47. Shamsher Singh Tript, 51. Tara Singh, 54. Dhunda Singh Kupi, 62. Hari Singh, 64. Waryam Singh Bhaand, 65. Hansa Singh, 67. Kirpal Singh Landa

...anchester), 73. Sewa Singh Mandla, 75. Natha
...ngh Advocate (Malaysia), 77. Nahar Singh
...dvocate (Kenya), 79. Gurcharan Singh Rathore,
... Krishna Singh Digwa, 83. Khazan Singh
...aker, 85. Kartar Singh, 86. Shingar Singh
...tiwal.

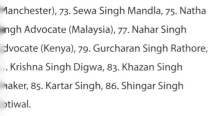

Right: Marriage of Narinder Singh Kapany to
Satinder Kaur at Maharajah Bhupinder Singh
Dharamsala, standing outside 79 Sinclair Road,
after their marriage ceremony 1954

for the Maharajah Bhupinder Singh Dharamsala, Kartar Singh Granthi being of one the first.

The earliest known marriage in Britain according to Sikh religious custom was that of Maharajah Jagatjit Singh's son, the Tikka Sahib Paramjit Singh in 1937. The heir apparent of Kapurthala married an English lady, Stella Mudge, who became his third wife. Formerly from Kent, she used the stage name of Estelle Alice and had been a dancer with the Folies-Bergère in Paris, and in London. The wedding ceremony was conducted at the Maharajah Bhupinder Singh Dharamsala in Shepherds Bush in July 1937[9] and the bride took the name Maharani Narinder Kaur Sahiba.[10]

Although the earliest wedding between two Sikhs was perhaps that of Makhan Singh Chand and Shakuntla Kaur in 1950, the ceremony was not conducted at Sinclair Road, but at the house of Makhan Singh Chand's father at Golden Street in London's East End, with the *Guru Granth Sahib* procured from the Dharamsala.[11] However, the

India's Ambassador to France Hardit Singh Malik visiting the Maharajah Bhupinder Singh Dharamsala, c. 1957

ft: Mrs Ajit Singh at the naming ceremony of er daughter Gagandeep Kaur at Maharajah nupinder Singh Dharamsala in 1957

wedding of Imperial College London student Narinder Singh Kapany to Satinder Kaur, an English literature student at the University of London, on 6 February 1954 was one of the earliest recorded at 79 Sinclair Road. Narinder Singh, who himself lived in Sinclair Road, two blocks from the Gurdwara, even hired a Rolls Royce for the plush occasion to collect the couple from the Maharajah Bhupinder Singh Dharamsala. The guests on this occasion were chiefly made up of friends and colleagues from Imperial College. Narinder Singh Kapany went on to successfully design equipment to make the first fibre assembly to demonstrate image transmission through flexible fibres.

In 1957, at the invitation of Dr Diwan Singh, the Akali leader Master Tara Singh visited England to obtain support and funding for his political party, and toured the Sikh community all over Britain, including in his visit the Dharamsala at Sinclair Road, the Midlands, and Manchester's Gurdwara in Monton Street, which had opened four years earlier.

The late 1950s saw a shift in the pattern of the management and involvement of Sikhs in the Khalsa Jatha British Isles. With the new Sikh communities migrating from Singapore and Malaysia, the

Naranjan Singh Binning's family wedding at the
Maharajah Bhupinder Singh Dharamsala, c. 1959

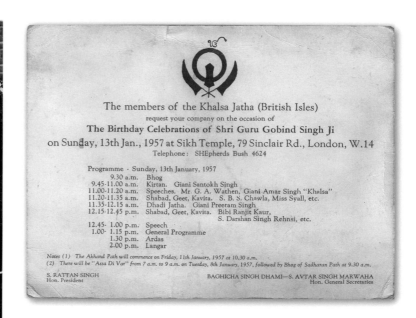

The members of the Khalsa Jatha (British Isles)
request your company on the occasion of
The Birthday Celebrations of Shri Guru Gobind Singh Ji
on Sunday, 13th Jan., 1957 at Sikh Temple, 79 Sinclair Rd., London, W.14
Telephone: SHEpherds Bush 4624

Programme · Sunday, 13th January, 1957
9.30 a.m.   Bhog
9.45-11.00 a.m.   Kirtan.   Giani Santokh Singh
11.00-11.20 a.m.   Speeches.   Mr. G. A. Wathen, Giani Amar Singh "Khalsa"
11.20-11.35 a.m.   Shabad, Geet, Kavita.   S. B. S. Chawla, Miss Syall, etc.
11.35-12.15 a.m.   Dhadi Jatha.   Giani Preetam Singh
12.15-12.45 p.m.   Shabad, Geet, Kavita.   Bibi Ranjit Kaur,
                                                   S. Darshan Singh Rehnsi, etc.

12.45- 1.00 p.m.   Speech
1.00- 1.15 p.m.   General Programme
1.30 p.m.   Ardas
2.00 p.m.   Langar

Notes (1)   The Akhand Path will commence on Friday, 11th January, 1957 at 10.30 a.m.
(2)   There will be "Assa Di Var" from 7 a.m. to 9 a.m. on Tuesday, 8th January, 1957, followed by Bhog of Sadharan Path at 9.30 a.m.

S. RATTAN SINGH   BAGHICHA SINGH DHAMI—S. AVTAR SINGH MARWAHA
Hon. President   Hon. General Secretaries

control of the Dharamsala came primarily to their hands, with a less active role played by the earlier Sikhs. This partly resulted from the opening of many new regional Gurdwaras for the established communities around Britain, who now began to dedicate their time to their local Gurdwaras while the new migrant community in West London congregated around the Maharajah Bhupinder Singh Dharamsala. However, old *sevaks* such as Asa Singh Grewal, Inder Singh Koori, Sarwan Singh and Pakher Singh gave their continued service.

Right: Khalsa Jatha invitation for the Birthday
celebrations of Guru Gobind Singh Ji,
January 1957

CHAPTER 6

Sant Fateh Singh laying the foundation
stone of the Central London Gurdwara on 11
September 1966

1960 – 1970

by Peter Bance

The 1960s saw a new era for the Khalsa Jatha British Isles, with an ev-
er-increasing Sikh population. The premises at 79 Sinclair Road were
becoming too small to house the growing congregation and the need
for a purpose-built location became apparent.

At a meeting held at the Dharamsala on 1 December 1963 it was
decided that a committee comprising Rawel Singh, Joginder Singh
Sandhu, Gurbachan Singh Sohal, Amrik Singh and Gurbachan Singh
Gill be nominated to raise funds for the purchase of a new Gurdwara
premises. In 1964 a piece of land and premises known as Norland Castle on Queensdale Road came on to the market and was purchased
by the Khalsa Jatha British Isles for £25,000 with the help of donations
from the *Sangat*.

ight: Sikh women and children preparing the
angar in the kitchen of Maharajah Bhupinder
Singh Dharamsala, c. 1965

SIKHS IGNORE SITE THREAT

Work starts on new temple

BY A STAFF REPORTER

Undeterred by the possibility of compulsory purchase of the site, 200 Sikhs, some carrying picks and shovels like ritual symbols, marched through Shepherds Bush, W., last night to start work on their new temple.

The Sikhs say that they have planning permission from the Royal Borough of Kensington and Chelsea. A Sikh leader said they intended to start work although they knew Hammersmith council might seek compulsory purchase of the site as part of a development plan.

The chanting crowd wove their way through the streets from their present temple in a house in Sinclair Road to the new site, a derelict Salvation Army citadel in Queensdale Road, half a mile away. There, a short religious ceremony invoking a blessing on their work was held on the steps where their leader Sant Fateh Singh laid a foundation stone last September.

With daylight fading, the Sikhs began attacking floorboards in the interior of the skeletal building and passing out pieces of wood to the waiting lines of helpers, some of them women, who piled them into giant bins standing in the road.

Hospital fears over

Sikhs at work yesterday in a
and build a temple on it, al

ion Army Citadel in Shepherds Bush, W.   They plan to clear the site
ersmith council may seek compulsory purchase of the site to use in a
development plan.

On 11 September 1966, Akali leader Sant Fateh Singh visited England from the Punjab. His visit was to gather support for his party and, like Master Tara Singh some years earlier, he too travelled the length of the country to meet the Sikh communities residing all over Britain. On the day of his arrival he was driven to the new development site at Queensdale Road, where he laid the foundation stone of the Central Gurdwara London at a special ceremony.[1] During the course of his stay in Britain, Sant Fateh Singh several times visited the Dharamsala at Sinclair Road, where he personally performed prayers for the masses.

Previous Page: Sikhs working at the Norland Castle site Queensdale Road, despite Hammersmith's Council's compulsory purchase order, April 10th 1967

The Norland Castle site was a derelict former Salvation Army. In 1967 Hammersmith Council sought a compulsory purchase order for the site to be used in a development plan, even though Kensington and Chelsea Council had earlier given planning permission to the Khalsa Jatha. Despite this, the Sikhs, undeterred by the possibility of the compulsory purchase, some 200 of them carrying picks and shovels, marched through Shepherds Bush on 9 April 1967 to start work on the new temple which would be named Central London Gurdwara.[2] The Council finally backed down and the Khalsa Jatha was victorious, completion of the Gurdwara building finally being allowed. On 12 April 1967 Hammersmith Council's compulsory purchase order for the Queensdale Road site was withdrawn at a council meeting, without any explanation. *The Times* reported that the Sikhs planned to hold a rally and service of thanksgiving at Ealing Town Hall on the following Sunday.[3]

Although the Maharajah Bhupinder Singh Dharamsala was the first Gurdwara in Britain, it was not registered until 1968. The first registered Sikh Temple was Manchester's Monton Street Gurdwara, in 1953.

The Central London Gurdwara (Khalsa Jatha) was registered as a charity on 11 April 1969 and the new Gurdwara on Queensdale Road was officially inaugurated on 7 December 1969, coinciding with the 500th Anniversary of Guru Nanak Dev's birth, amid great celebrations all around the world. The former Dharamsala building at 79 Sinclair Road was kept on by the Khalsa Jatha, and remained as a functioning Gurdwara, with a *Guru Granth Sahib* installed, until the building was sold in 1980.

Above: Sant Fateh Singh reciting from the Guru Granth Sahib at 79 Sinclair Road, with Preetam Singh, QC, standing and holding a flywhisk, 1966

*The Ranjit Nagara which sounded the inauguration of the Festiva[l]
India on March 22, at the Royal Festival Hall was presented by the [H]*
Commissioner, Dr. V.A. Seyid Muhammad (above) to Mr. P.S. M[o]
president of the Central Gurudwara, Shepherds Bush, at a functio[n]
India House in the presence of Dr. Gopal Singh, the chairman of
Minorities Commission, and representatives of the Khalsa Jatna, Br[itish]
Isles.

resentation of the Ranjit Nagara (drum of
ictory) to Prakash Singh Maini, India Weekly
ewspaper

1970 – 2008

by Gurpreet Singh Anand

Shortly after acquisition of the new Gurdwara at 62 Queensdale Road, the building was severely damaged by fire. The Khalsa Jatha received a substantial payout from its insurers and this contributed to full re-payment of the bank loan used for the purchase. Work on restoring the damaged Gurdwara building began and was funded by generous donations from the public.

In 1980 the Khalsa Jatha purchased the two houses next door to the Gurdwara, numbers 58 and 60 Queensdale Road with the assis-tance of Jagmail Singh Gill. These houses were in a derelict state and, following complete refurbishment, they were put to use to provide quarters for the *Granthis* and *Raagis*. Other rooms were made into classrooms and the Khalsa Jatha was able to expand its education facilities for teaching Punjabi and Sikh history. The Khalsa Jatha re-mained a centre for Sikh activities of national importance and played a leading role in representing Sikh interests within the UK and be-yond.

In 1980 a tape recording library was started in earnest by Amarjit Singh Paul on behalf of the Gurdwara. Working late in to the night, tape recordings of the prior week's *kirtan* were duplicated and made available to the *sangat* the following week. This *sewa* is now under-taken by Manmohan Singh Sohanpal and Manmander Singh Sohan-pal and family. Through their collective efforts they have successfully grown the library into one of the UK's largest *kirtan* resources with *kirtan* now available on both CD and video tape.

On 22 March 1982 a Ranjit Nagara (drum of victory) was sounded for the inauguration of the Festival of India. Later the same day the

Ranjit Nagara was presented to Prakash Singh Maini, the President of the Khalsa Jatha, by the Indian High Commissioner, Dr V. A. Seyid Muhammad. A Ranjit Nagara was first prepared for Guru Gobind Singh in 1684 and was sounded every day at Takht Kesgarh Sahib[1] as a sign of Sikh sovereignty.[2]

In June 1984 the Khalsa Jatha assumed a leading role in representing the sentiments of the Sikh community, when it was involved in organising a mass protest in response to the military attack on the Akal Takht and The Golden Temple.

The protest took place on 10 June 1984, when more than 25,000 protestors marched from Hyde Park to Smithfield Market via India House.[3] The Khalsa Jatha set up large marquees at Hyde Park where they provided *langar* for the protestors.

Subsequently the Khalsa Jatha found itself in a hotbed of international Sikh political activity. The Khalsa Jatha hosted a conference of Sikh leaders which was also attended by Afghans to show their solidarity with the Sikhs, as they were fighting to liberate their country from Soviet occupation.

In the midst of all this activity the then President of the Jatha, Manjit Singh Selhi, found himself banned from visiting India along with many other prominent Sikh leaders. These bans were later lifted. Following the anti-Sikh riots and pogroms of November 1984 in India, many Sikhs fled from India and the Khalsa Jatha saw many refugees form part of the congregation. Many had horrific accounts of how they had escaped the anti-Sikh riots in India.

In 1986 the Khalsa Jatha opened a youth centre in order to encourage young Sikhs to play a wider role in society. The youth centre was very successful and arranged seminars that discussed a wide range of issues affecting young Sikhs in the UK. The Khalsa Jatha also participated in Sport Aid, organised by Bob Geldof, and members of the Jatha participated in the Sport Aid run in Central London on 25 May 1986.

During the late 1980s a small second hall was created from the balcony in the main hall of the Gurdwara, thereby enabling more functions to be held. This hall was extended in 2001 during a phase of major refurbishment. That year also saw the Gurdwara used as the location for the wedding scene in Gurinder Chadha's blockbuster movie *Bend it Like Beckham*. The filming of the marriage created a real dilemma for the management of the Khalsa Jatha, as it felt that if the two actors went through the complete marriage ceremony in front of the *Guru Granth Sahib*, then in its eyes they would be actually married. The Khalsa Jatha was able to agree a way forward with Gurinder Chadha that allowed the filming to happen in such a way that a Sikh

Gurnam Singh Sahni and Jagjit Singh Chohan at a 'Khalistan' rally at Hyde Park, 1984

Khalsa Jatha youth participating in the
Sport Aid run, 1986

marriage ceremony did not actually take place.

In 1994 the Central Gurdwara started publication of a newsletter called the *Sikh Spirit* which contained items on Sikh history, spirituality and news. This led to the creation of a web page and the Khalsa Jatha became the first Gurdwara with a presence on the internet. The Khalsa Jatha to this day continues to publish a monthly newsletter.

In 2005 a controversial decision by the then management committee threatened the very existence of the Gurdwara and would have seen the premises relocated to West Ealing. This would have resulted in the disappearance of the only Central London-located Gurdwara and it was met with outrage from the whole UK Sikh community. This move was successfully prevented and the Queensdale Road site was saved.

The Gurdwara has become a resource for the wider community, playing host to over fifty school visits each year and providing accommodation for Sikh students and visitors to London.

CHAPTER 8

The *Next* 100 Years

by Sukhbinder Singh Paul

From humble beginnings to the present day, the Central Gurdwara London owes its existence to the vision and determination of the founding fathers of the Khalsa Jatha British Isles. As foreign settlers in a foreign land, they stood firm in their religious beliefs and sought to cement their bond with their newly adopted country by establishing the first Dharamsala in Europe.

The Central Gurdwara London in its present form has become more than just four walls, for it has come to embody the spirit of Sikhism, providing a beacon of light to all those seeking sanctuary, solace and spiritual peace.

Throughout its evolution and its many forms, the present-day Gurdwara has been a focal point for Sikhs and non-Sikhs alike. For the early Sikh migrants, nobility, convalescing soldiers of the Great War, freedom fighters, eminent businessmen, professionals and the wider community, the Gurdwara has been a meeting place that has connected all those who walk through its doors.

As well as fulfilling its central role as a place of worship the Gurdwara has also evolved into a place of learning, with Punjabi, *kirtan*, kirtan library, martial arts, *gurmat* camps, sports classes and a proposed Sikh museum forming part of its activities. In these endeavours future generations are encouraged to carry on the vision and ideology of the founding fathers into the next century, instilling within them the sense of belonging and community pride that these Sikhs had fought so hard to establish.

Glossary

Adi Granth The name of the Sikh holy book prior to attaining the status of Guru

Akhand Path Full, non-stop recital of the Guru Granth Sahib, which normally takes forty-eight hours

Amrit The sweet water used in the ceremony of baptism, also known as Pahul

Amrit parchaar The promotion and initiation of the baptism ceremony

Ayahs Indian nanny or nursemaid

Bhat/Bhatra Sikh sub-group of travelling bards

Deewan Congregational hall or gathering; or a royal court

Dharamsala Hostel, shelter or free living abode

Dholaki Double-sided drum

Durbar Prayer hall in a Gurdwara

Giani/Gyani Sikh priest or qualified learned person

Granthi Reader of the Guru Granth Sahib at a Gurdwara

Gurbani Extracts from the Guru Granth Sahib

Gurdwara A Sikh Temple or place of worship

Gurmat Advice of the Guru(s)

Gurmukhi The Sikh script of the Punjabi language

Gurpurabs Religious days celebrated on important dates connected with the Sikh Gurus

Guru Granth Sahib The Sikh Holy Scriptures

Gutka A small-sized book containing chosen hymns or prayers from the Sikh Scriptures

Jaito Morcha The movement to consolidate all of the historic Sikh Gurdwaras under a single Sikh body

Jat A sub-caste of agriculturalists

Khalsa Pure; one who has been baptised by Amrit/Pahul

Kirtan Singing of hymns

Langar The free Community Kitchen found at every Gurdwara

Lascars Indian sailors

Miri-piri Temporal (miri) and spiritual (piri) authority introduced by Guru Hargobind

Nishan Sahib The flagpole outside a Gurdwara. The flagpole is wrapped in saffron cloth, with the Sikh emblem on the very top

Parchaar Preaching

Raagi One who conduct and sings hymns and prayers

Sangat Community; a congregation or gathering of Sikhs

Sant Sikh holy man

Saropa Honour in recognition or deed

Sewa/Seva Voluntary service

Sewadar Volunteering services free of charge to the community

Shabad kirtan Recitation of religious hymns

Shabads Sikh hymns

Vaaja Musical instrument similar to a harmonium

Vaisakhi Sikh New Year, the day on which the Khalsa was formed in 1699

Notes

CHAPTER 1

Professor Ganga Singh travelled to Europe and the USA to spread the word of Sikhism but returned as a Europeanised gentleman.

Downing College Archives, Cambridge University.

Cambridge University Archives, ref: Graduati 32/34; Min. VIII.62.

Downing College Archives, Cambridge.

Cambridge University Archives, ref: Graduati 32/34; Min. VIII.62.

According to University London Archives, a Sikh student by the name of Mr Teja Singh registered at University College in October 1910. He passed his 'Sp Intern Engl' in 1911 and was awarded a pass in his BSc in English (Hons) in 1913. [Richard Temple, Archivist, Senate House Library, University of London].

The Times, 17 January 1910.

Visram, Rozina, Asians in Britain: 400 Years History, London, Pluto Press, 2002, p. 104.

Visram, Rozina, Ayahs, Lascars and Princes, London, Pluto Press, 1986, p. 106.

). Teja Singh MA, LLB, AM (Harvard), later became known as Sant Teja Singh Mastuana.

. Hardit Singh Malik was appointed CIE in 1941, OBE in 1938, and Grand Officer of the Légion d'Honneur in 1952.

. The Times, 16 October 1982.

. The Times, 5 February 1953.

CHAPTER 2

1. Sahni, Gurnam Singh, History of Khalsa Jatha British Isles (Punjabi Translation), 1985, p. 4.

2. The Times, 'Proposed Sikh Church in London', 3 July 1911.

3. Cited in the Amended version of the Constitution, as approved by the General Body of the Central London Gurdwara on 29 December 1985.

4. The members of the Khalsa Jatha were: Sant Teja Singh, Maan Singh LLB, Teja Singh Bsc (London), Narain Singh Sargodha, Basheshar Singh BA (Canterbury), Atma Singh AACI (Engineer), Shivdev Singh Oberai (Sialkot), Malik Teja Singh Bsc (London), Kahn Singh Nabha, Subedar-Major Gurdit Singh (Amritsar), Professor Puran Singh, Sadhu Singh E.A. Conservator (Forests), Narotam Singh, a barrister-atlLaw, and Darshan Singh Vahali.

5. The Jatha from the USA and Canada started from Akal Takht on 2 January 1925 and on 17 January they arrived at Jaito, where they were arrested.

6. Anon., '47th Sikhs Great War Records', typescript, p. 59 [Collection of Peter Bance].

7. Illustrated London News, 'How India Helped in The War', by Princess Sophia Duleep Singh, 21 September 1918.

8. The Times, 'Wounded Indians to See London', 24 December 1914.

CHAPTER 3

1. *The Times*, 'Sikh Deputation', 11 August 1920.
2. *The Times*, 'Funeral of Shiv Dev Singh', 29 December 1932.
3. In 1930, Manmohan Singh had competed for the £500 prize given by the Aga Khan for an Indian accomplishing a solo flight between England and India. Manmohan Singh made two attempts. His first flight was on 24 January 1930, when he took off from Croydon, but was forced to land in thick fog on a mountain road in southern Italy. His second attempt also had to be abandoned midway. On his third attempt he took off from Croydon on 8 April 1930 and reached Karachi, but not within the stipulated period of one month, losing time owing to a forced landing he had to make in a swamp near Marseilles. Manmohan Singh missed the prize, but he became the first to complete a solo flight from England to India. In 1934–35, Manmohan Singh accomplished another solo journey in a light aircraft, again the first by an Indian, from England to South Africa. He died in action at Singapore in 1942.
4. Jullandhar, Hoshiarpur and Ludhiana are major districts in the Punjab.
5. Visram, *Asians in Britain*, p. 255.
6. Dr Diwan Singh (1894–1983), had participated in the infamous 'Guru Ka Bagh Morcha' of 1921 in British India, where hundreds of peaceful Sikh demonstrators were mercilessly beaten every day by the police. In 1931 Diwan Singh enrolled at Edinburgh Medical University to qualify to practise as a doctor in Britain. A year later he joined Queen Elizabeth Medical School in Birmingham, and became the first Sikh doctor, perhaps the first Indian doctor, in Britain.
7. Asa Singh Grewal settled in London in 1932, peddling gentlemen's accessories, and later trading at the markets of Ladbroke Grove, Hammersmith and London's East End. In addition, in 1938 he played the role of a Bengal Lancer in Korda's third Empire Film, *The Drum*, which starred 'Sabu'. Asa Singh was joined by his family and son Sajjan Singh in 1952.
8. Tarlok Singh worked in the Indian Civil Service (ICS).
9. Flight Officer Manmohan Singh was in England in 1934, attempting to accomplish another solo journey by an Indian in a light aircraft from England to South Africa.

10. 10. Kaval Malik was the daughter of Hardit Singh Malik' older brother, Sir Teja Singh Malik. Kaval's brothe Shubehintan Singh was also in England, studying agricultur at a college in Kent.
11. Singh, Sikander, *Udham Singh Alias Ram Mohammed Sing Azad*, Amritsar, Chattar Singh Jiwan Singh Publishers, 199 pp. 90–1.
12. *The Times*, 'Anniversary of Guru Gobind Singh', 21 Januar 1937.
13. The Ghaddar Party was a US and Canadian-base organisation founded in 1913 with the aim of liberatin India from British rule.
14. 14 Artillery Passage was a popular Indian lodging abov Grewal-Bassi's grocery store in the East End of London.
15. In July 1939, Udham Singh was living in Southampton 12 Manchester Street, while working at Messrs Lindsa Parkinson and Co. Limited, contracted as a carpenter. September 1939 he had moved to 581 Wimbourne Roa Winton, Bournemouth and as working at Blandford Milit Camp as a carpenter. Singh, Sikander, *Udham Singh Ali Ram Mohammed Singh Azad*, Amritsar, Chattar Sing Jiwan Singh Publishers, 1998, pp.170–3.
16. Sahni, Gurnam Singh, *History of Khalsa Jatha British Isl* (Punjabi Translation), 1985, p. 7.

CHAPTER 4

1. *The Times*, 'Farewell Party to Mohan Singh', 24 Februar 1940.
2. Shaad, Rattan S., *Sangat Bhatra De Kratik Laher Da Ithi* Patiala, Phulkian Press, 1982, p. 19.
3. Subash Chander Bose was the one of the leaders of th Indian Independence Movement, and later led the India National Army against the British Raj in the Second Wor War.
4. When partition became inevitable and congre factionalism began to assert itself in 1947, he flew India and actively pursued the possibility of a Sikh Sta with Master Tara Singh and the Maharajah of Patiala. 1960, Pandit Nehru offered Dr Diwan Singh the post Ambassador to Ethiopia. Characteristically, Dr Diwa

Singh refused and told the Prime Minister of India 'thank you for the offer but how can I accept such an honour from a government that is daily throwing hundreds of my brothers and sisters into the gaol?'

The house had initially been chosen by the Changa Bhatra Naujwan Sabha UK, as its temporary Head Office, from 1940 to November 1946, as 8 Golding Street was under the threat of fierce London bombing during the war.

Shaad, *Sangat Bhatra*, p. 36.

HAPTER 5

Bhagat Singh was hanged on the 23rd March 1931, along with his colleagues Sukhdev and Rajguru, for the murder of J. P. Saunders, an Assistant Superintendent of Police in Lahore.

Singh, Harbans, *Encyclopedia of Sikhism*, Patiala, Punjab University, 1998, Vol. I, p. 31.

Shaad, *Sangat Bhatra*, p. 144.

Ajit Singh left England and sadly died on the day of India's Independence on the 15 August 1947 from heart failure.

Shaad, *Sangat Bhatra*, pp.142–5.

Shaad, *Sangat Bhatra*, p. 17.

Shaad, *Sangat Bhatra*, pp. 16–18.

The Parkarma is the square walkway around the Golden Temple at Amritsar.

'Khalsa Jatha British Isles' leaflet, August 1950; family papers in the possession of Abinash Singh Taak.

Courtesy of Christopher J. Buyers.

Stella [Astella] Mudge was the second daughter of Joseph Mudge, a wire-walker and publican of Bow and Bromley, Kent, by his wife, Mrs Emily Mudge MBE, from a farming family of Ilkley, Yorkshire. Died in Delhi on 23 February 1984 and buried at the Prithviraj Road Cemetery.

Courtesy of Makhan Singh Chand.

CHAPTER 6

1. *The Times*, 12 September 1966.
2. *The Times*, 10 April 1967.
3. *The Times*, 13 April 1967.

CHAPTER 7

1. Takhat Kesgarh Sahib is also known as Anandpur Sahib and is the place where the Sikhs were initiated into the Khalsa by Guru Gobind Singh in 1699.
2. *India Weekly*, 17 June 1982.
3. *The Times*, 11 June 1984.

Acknowledgements

Central Gurdwara, London, would like to thank everyone who made this book possible, in particular the following people who gave their invaluable support and contribution, including Bhupinder Singh Bhasin for his support and advice, Juga Singh (GRFIK.COM) for his expertise, advice, design and typesetting. We would also like to thank Gurbachan Singh Sidhu for his assistance on the history of the Guru Granth Sahib. Judith Opprenheimer for editing the work, Jasprit Singh for photographing the Gurdwara, and finally the current Central Gurdwara Committee for their support throughout this project.

We also like to thank the following individuals and organisations, without whose contribution, resources and archives, this book would not have been complete: Abinash Singh Taak who made available his family archives and photographs of the last 60 years, Dr Indarjit Singh OBE for the Dharamsala's early history, Mr and Mrs Harbans Singh for their invaluable resources, Mrs Jasjit Kaur Selhi, Mrs Gian Kaur Chadha, Mr Jagmail Singh Gill, Mr Jaspal Singh Anand, Kushwant Singh (New Delhi), Gurnam Singh Sahni, Rozina Visram for the background history, Cambridge University Archives and the National Archives, Kew.

We would also like to thank the following for generously supporting this book; Kuljit Singh Gulati, Rajinder Singh Bhasin, Raj Singh Narula, Rajinder Singh Baksh, Bhai Bhagwant Singh, Jasjit Kaur Selhi, Charanjit Singh, Gurbachan Singh Gill, Madan Singh Khurana (in memory of his wife Davinder Kaur Khurana), Narinder Singh Sawhney, Manmohan Singh Sohanpal, Joginder Singh Gujral and Darshan Singh Sadana.